McTar Petroleum Co. Ltd.

GREATER
VANCOUVER

Sunset over Vancouver, Strait of Georgia and Vancouver Island from Mount Seymour

Overleaf: **Spring Evening on Kitsilano Beach**

GREATER
VANCOUVER
DOUGLAS LEIGHTON

ALTITUDE

Canadian Rockies/Vancouver

PUBLICATION INFORMATION

Canadian Cataloguing in Publication Data
Leighton, Douglas, 1953-
Greater Vancouver
ISBN 1-55153-058-9
1. Lower Mainland(B.C.) – Pictorial Works.   2. Vancouver
Metropolitan Area (B.C.) – Pictorial Works.   I. Title.
FC3845.L69L44 1995   971.1'3304'0222   C94-910971-1
F1089.L79L44 1995

Edited by Yvonne Van Ruskenveld
Designed by Stephen Hutchings
Electronic page layout by Alison Barr and Sandra Davis
Map by Catherine Burgess
Financial management by Laurie Smith

**This book is dedicated
to Constance and Stuart Ostlund
whose help and encouragement made it all possible.**

Made in Western Canada
Printed and bound in Western Canada by Friesen Printers, Altona, Manitoba.

Altitude GreenTree Program
Altitude Publishing will plant in Canada twice as many trees as were used in
the manufacturing of this book.

Altitude Publishing Canada Ltd.
The Canadian Rockies
P.O. Box 1410, Canmore Alberta T0L 0M0

"Symphony of Fire" above English Bay

CONTENTS

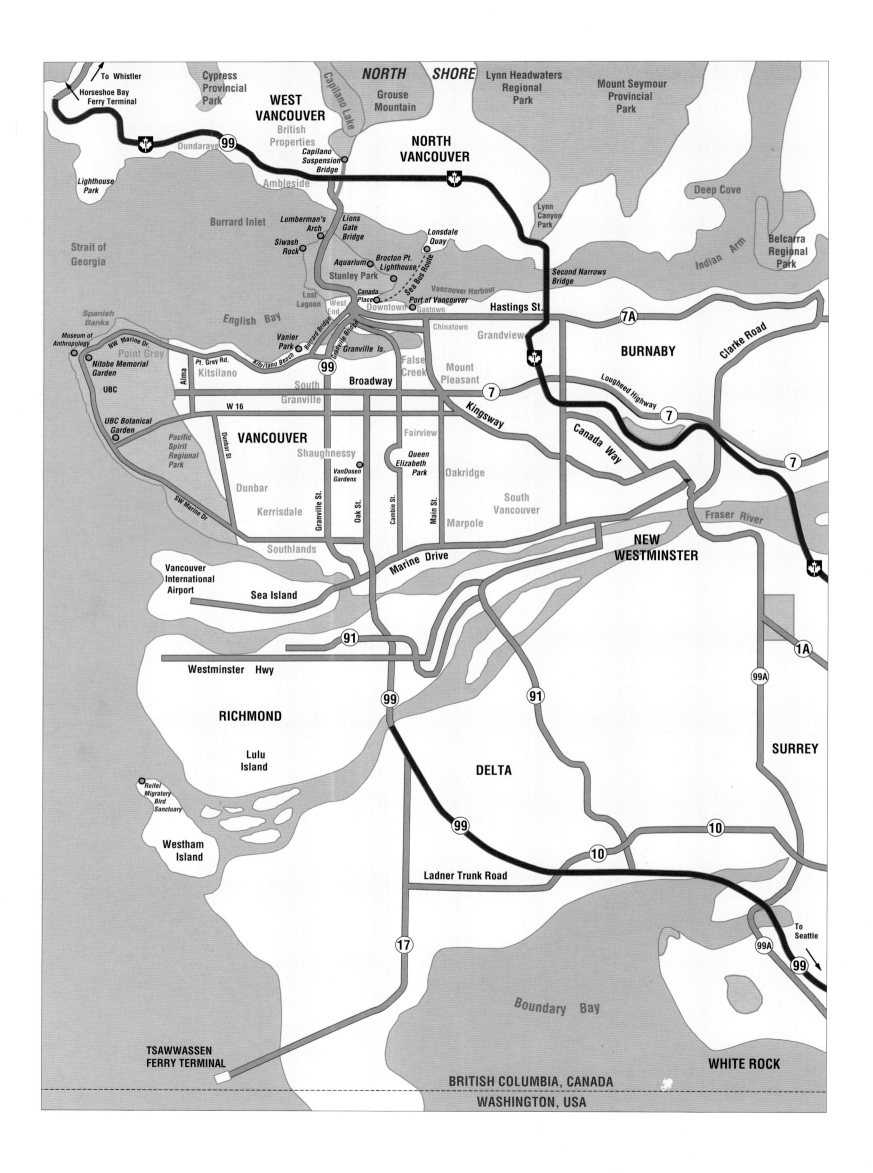

VANCOUVER

Vancouver is a city whose time has come. In this era of trade, technology and travel, Vancouver is ideally placed in geography and time. Greater Vancouver is the fastest growing region on the continent and is home to the largest North American port on the booming Pacific Rim. It is close to the Canada-United States border, and office hours here overlap with those in the United States, Europe and Asia.

Vancouver offers a unique quality of life and a marvelously mild climate. Tourists, retirees and the wealthy have long been attracted to Vancouver's ocean and mountain views, and the easy availability of sailing, skiing, seawall walks and sandy beaches. Vancouverites enjoy a clean, safe and vibrantly multicultural Canadian city.

Residents of eastern Canadian cities, understandably jealous of their popular sister, like to talk about "rainy Vancouver." The lushness of this garden city is beautiful evidence that it does rain. Downtown Vancouver gets about 150 centimetres of precipitation, mostly in the winter, but only an average of 60 centimetres of this is snow. Weather patterns generate weeks of grey winter days and long sunny summers.

The northwest coast of North America was one of the last frontiers to be explored by Europeans. For at least 8000 years, Native peoples had this fertile ecosystem to themselves. Food was abundant, from berries and deer to salmon and mussels. Warm in their cedar winter houses, Natives developed ingenious tools and technologies and created inspired art.

Then another world arrived. In July 1791, looking for the legendary Northwest Passage, Spanish mariners from California landed on Point Grey for a night. The following June, Captain George Vancouver, settling British claims to this coast, entered Burrard Inlet where he was greeted by canoes of Coast Salish, eager to trade.

In 1858 thousands of Americans led the gold rush on the Fraser River and stirred the British to establish the colony of British Columbia, with its capital at New Westminster. While surveying Burrard Inlet for naval bases, they explored the astonishing temperate rain forest of gigantic conifers. Logging began in 1862, and soon Burrard Inlet lumber was world renowned. In 1867 "Gassy Jack" Deighton opened a saloon outside Stamp's lumber mill. "Gastown," a rough and tumble town, grew around it. Today, Gastown is a small corner of downtown Vancouver.

In 1871 British Columbia joined Canada on the promise that a transcontinental railway would be built. As the Canadian Pacific Railway neared completion in 1884, manager William Van Horne arrived at Burrard Inlet. He foresaw that this key port was "destined to be a great city" and found the ideal site at the new townsite of Granville — which everyone still called Gastown. For the future city he envisioned, he insisted on the name "Vancouver."

Vancouver was incorporated on April 6, 1886, and on June 13, a fire roared through the wooden buildings of the town. From these ashes, rose a new kind of city, planned and modern from the start. Van Horne, already instrumental in the creation of Canada's Rocky Mountain national parks, knew that Vancouver's spectacular setting would make it an international tourist attraction. Even the visionary Van Horne would be astonished to see just how right he was.

DOUGLAS LEIGHTON

Overleaf: **Vancouver, Burrard Inlet, North Shore Mountains**

DOWNTOWN

Gateway at Chinese Cultural Centre

This traditional ornate gateway was made in China and displayed at Expo 86 before becoming a landmark in today's Chinatown. More than 250,000 people of Chinese heritage now live in Greater Vancouver.

Left: **Lunch Entertainer, Park Place**

Summer downtown is especially lively at lunch, as office workers pour out into the many green public spaces and restaurant patios. In this treed courtyard beneath Burrard Street towers, a series of noon performances takes place against a backdrop of stepped waterfalls.

DOWNTOWN

One of the most striking images of Vancouver is the city's downtown skyline set against the North Shore mountains—the contrast of high-rise density and wilderness space. This city in the mountains, with water on three sides, has nowhere to grow but up. As early as 1912, it boasted the two tallest buildings in the British Empire, and now with 170,000 people working downtown and another 60,000 expected within a decade, the skyline is pushing higher.

Despite this growth, Vancouver is the only major North American city without a freeway to its downtown core. A freeway system was proposed in the 1960s, but it would have destroyed both Gastown and Chinatown, the historic heart of the city. Vancouverites chose culture over convenience, and to make the most of what they saved, began heritage restoration and community revitalization in Gastown in 1969.

Most downtown workers commute from suburbs by car, bus, or SkyTrain rapid transit or from North Vancouver by SeaBus. But the 60,000 people who live in downtown Vancouver can simply walk to work. Across Burrard Street from the office towers are the high-rises of the West End. Bordered by English Bay, Stanley Park and Coal Harbour, and within walking distance of all that downtown has to offer, this choice location is the most densely populated neighbourhood in Canada.

Downtown has much to offer. It's compact, and with so many people living here, it stays lively long after office hours. At lunch the cellular-phone crowd shares the city's many outdoor spaces with tourists wandering off Robson Street, shoppers from the suburbs and residents out for a coffee on a sidewalk patio. You can walk safely anywhere downtown — to an international smorgasbord of restaurants, theatres, galleries, nightclubs, street festivals and sports events.

This cosmopolitan mix is an endless theatre for people watchers, and there's always the chance of seeing celebrities. Vancouver has become the third largest film and television production centre in North America, and the city's fertile creative scene is buzzing. Film makers love the Vancouver area for the diversity of locations it offers: city, mountains, water and even "Wild West" out in the Fraser Valley.

Although most of today's West Enders wonder why anyone would live anywhere else, the first residents were called fools for settling here in 1862. Three discouraged prospectors, John Morton, Sam Brighouse and William Hailstone, saw more promise in the clay deposits of Coal Harbour than in the gold fields of the Fraser and claimed the land from Burrard Street to Stanley Park. They were ridiculed in New Westminster as "the three greenhorns" for their plans to make bricks when they were surrounded by the world's best lumber and for paying $555.75 for this remote 225-hectare homestead. Their wisdom was proven later when Vancouver burned down in 1886 and these lands became some of the most valuable real estate in Canada.

In the summer of 1888, Dean Carmichael, a visitor to Vancouver, wrote: "Everywhere there are evidences of life and energy and vigor. In fact the streets thrill with signs of determination to push on and make Vancouver ... a great Canadian city binding the east and the west of the world together." In downtown Vancouver, you can still feel this energy.

Dusk Falls on Downtown Skyline

The twin peaks of The Lions (1629 metres) stand out on the North Shore mountains, a dramatic backdrop to Vancouver's skyline. In the foreground, the venerable, castle-like Hotel Vancouver is crowded by upstart office towers.

Entrance to the Marine Building

Downtown architecture is eclectic, reflecting the city's cosmopolitan roots and historic eras. This ornate Burrard Street portal was carefully restored in 1989. Its marvelously crafted art deco details symbolize the port city's marine heritage.

Right: **Moonrise over Coal Harbour from Stanley Park**

Little more than a century ago, the Squamish people who camped here would watch the moon rise over a dark, silent forest of giant trees.

The Sails of Canada Place

These huge teflon-coated sails have become the Vancouver waterfront's most distinctive architectural landmark. The busy seaplane base in Coal Harbour serves the south coast of the mainland, Vancouver Island and Seattle.

Left: Cruise Ship Docked at Canada Place

The daring architects who designed this landmark as Canada's national pavilion at Expo 86 sought to create a stylized ship. Today it is a busy cruise ship port and home to the World Trade Centre, the lavish Pan Pacific Hotel, a convention centre and an IMAX theatre. This site was once the Canadian Pacific pier that greeted the luxurious Empress ships sailing from Asia.

Gastown Steam Clock

Visitors to Gastown gather on the corner of Water and Cambie streets to watch the workings of the world's first steam clock and listen to its steam whistle rendition of London's Big Ben every 15 minutes. It looks as if it has been here since Gassy Jack's days, but it was built in 1977.

Left: **Vancouver Docks, Second Narrows Bridge**

Vancouver is the largest port, by volume, on the west side of the Pacific Rim and the largest wheat port in the world. This high tech container port is on the downtown's working east shore. The distant peaks are in Golden Ears Provincial Park.

Dr. Sun Yat-Sen Classical Chinese Garden

Adjacent to the Chinese Cultural Centre, this replica of a Ming Dynasty (1368-1644) walled retreat is the only full-scale classical garden ever built outside China. A joint project of the Chinese and Canadian governments, it was built with traditional techniques and materials by a team led by 52 artisans from Suzhou, China's "Garden City."

Chinese New Year

Vancouver's loud and colourful Chinese New Year parade through Chinatown is the highlight of 15 days of celebrations beginning on the last day of the last lunar month: late January to early February.

Vancouver Skyline on Coal Harbour

The docks of the Royal Vancouver Yacht Club float below the downtown towers.

Right: **Reflections of the Marine Building in the Daon Building**

Built at the end of the Roaring Twenties, this magnificent monument to the city's great expectations was conceived by its architects to be "a great marine rock rising from the sea, clinging with sea flora and fauna."

The Downtown Business Core

With computer screens filled with market data from around the world, Vancouver's Howe Street district has become a diversified Pacific Rim financial centre.

Left: **Robson Square**

Rising above the downtown civic square are the Vancouver Art Gallery (originally the 1912 provincial court house), the Hotel Vancouver and Cathedral Place, the city's modern (1991) answer to the Marine Building.

Stormy Sunset on English Bay

The West End's beaches are just minutes away from thousands of high-rise apartments. Sharing this shore with other Canadians escaping colder climates is this Inuit sculpture *InukShuk*, a gift from the government of the Northwest Territories.

Right: **Sunset over Coal Harbour and Stanley Park**

This view looks down over the Waterfront Centre Hotel and the glowing red dome atop the Pan Pacific Hotel at Canada Place.

West End, Sunset Beach

Although many West Enders can live without a car, some can't do without a boat. The odd "canoe" is a Chinese dragon boat, its crew practising for the annual Canadian International Dragon Boat Festival races held on False Creek.

Right: **Harbour Centre and Grouse Mountain**

Revolving every 90 minutes, the restaurant and viewing deck housed in this space-age tower offer spectacular 360° panoramas of downtown and its setting. Getting there — a one-minute, 167-metre zoom up in a glass elevator — is half the fun. In the spring, skiers on Grouse Mountain in the background can watch sailboats on the sparkling waters of English Bay.

STANLEY PARK

Canada Geese on Lost Lagoon

The waterfowl wintering here have been urbanized since feeding programs began with the declaration of a wildlife sanctuary in 1938. Now, with even more handouts from park visitors, they have formed a honking, quacking "waterfowl city" with population densities to rival the West End.

Left: **Giant Western Red Cedar and Douglas Fir**

Stanley Park holds a last remnant of the great forest that once covered what is now Greater Vancouver. The cedar was a precious resource for Native people, who used its durable, workable wood for dugout canoes, winter plankhouses, boxes, tools and carvings. Cedar bark strips were woven into hats, clothing and baskets.

STANLEY PARK

When Vancouverites want to show off their city to visitors, their favourite destination is Stanley Park, one of the largest and finest urban parks in the world. The seawall and road that circumnavigate this 405-hectare peninsula between English Bay and Burrard Inlet offer a sensational condensed tour of the city: views across Lost Lagoon to the West End, across Coal Harbour to the downtown waterfront and, from the Brockton Point lighthouse, a Burrard Inlet panorama that sweeps from the cruise ships at Canada Place, past Burnaby and around to North and West Vancouver at the foot of the North Shore mountains. West of the Lions Gate Bridge, seabirds nest on the rocky cliffs of Prospect Point, and bald eagles nest in the big trees above the west shore's sandy beaches with their sunset views across Georgia Strait to Vancouver Island.

Vancouver has been showing off Stanley Park since 1886. The park's creation was one of the first acts of Vancouver's first city council, pushed by the Canadian Pacific Railway both to enhance the value of the real estate they were developing in the West End and to encourage tourism. Almost overnight, Stanley Park became a genteel playground, with buggy-loads of tourists having their photographs taken within the trunk of a famous huge cedar, still there today.

For generations before Captain George Vancouver met the Coast Salish here in 1792, this peninsula was an important Native summer camp called Khwaykhway. A midden (refuse site) of discarded mussel shells near today's Lumberman's Arch was 2.5 metres deep, indicating thousands of years of occupation.

Even in a city full of parks, gardens and beaches, and surrounded by awesome natural beauty, Stanley Park stands out as Vancouver's most precious natural asset. Here, almost in the shadow of the downtown towers, is an oasis of the wild nature that once covered the city, and still surrounds it. Stressed executives and harried rush-hour commuters need only look out their windows to be soothed by the lush rainforest.

A visit to the park is even more soothing. On a hot summer day, the park is about 4 °C cooler than the concrete downtown core, and there are endless ways to enjoy the fresh ocean air. Circumnavigate the park offshore by tour boat or onshore by horse-drawn buggy or touring trolley. The seawall on a sunny afternoon is crowded with strollers, joggers, roller-bladers, cyclists, photographers, birdwatchers, artists and sedate souls on sandy beaches or shoreline benches. There are children's playgrounds and picnic areas, a cricket oval and lawn bowling greens, totem poles, statues and monuments, manicured flower gardens and quiet trails through stands of giant trees to secluded forest lakes.

One of the park's most popular attractions is the Vancouver Aquarium, which opened in 1950. Supported by admittance fees and over 55,000 members, it is one of the world's leading marine display and research facilities.

Vancouverites jealously guard their park. Apart from the road through to the Lions Gate Bridge, all serious threats to its integrity have been fiercely resisted. Now even minor changes are subject to heated public discussion, and the necessary replacement or upgrading of the Lions Gate Bridge promises to be a monumental civic debate.

Right: **Stanley Park and Downtown from Lions Gate Bridge**

March Daffodils, Stanley Park Gardens

This manicured portion of the park blooms through spring and summer. In the adjacent Rose Garden, 5000 bushes bloom in June.

Right: **Rhododendrons**

Vancouver has a love affair with flowers, especially rhododendrons. Many rhododendron species originate in mild, moist south Asian mountains and find ideal growing conditions here.

Face-to-Face with a Beluga Whale

The aquarium's underwater viewing rooms allow visitors to see belugas, orcas, dolphins, seals and sea otters in their natural element. The belugas squeal and chatter to each other as they curiously eye their human observers, making visitors wonder: Just what are they saying about us?

Left: **Orca at Vancouver Aquarium**

Canada's largest aquarium was one of the first in the world to exhibit killer whales (orcas), helping change public fear into concerned fascination. Although they no longer perform show tricks, these highly intelligent and social mammals still amuse themselves by splashing the crowds gathered to watch them. Wild orcas occasionally enter Burrard Inlet.

Jogger on the Seawall, Coal Harbour

Running forever in bronze is Vancouver's Harry Jerome, 1964 Olympic sprint medalist and world record holder.

Right: **Totem Poles at Brockton Point**

One of Vancouver's favourite photo opportunities, these colourful totems stand on the site of a traditional Coast Salish summer camp. However, they represent the monumental art of Native peoples who lived further north on the coast.

Making Rain in Vancouver

Stanley Park is just one of many locations that have helped make Vancouver the continent's third largest film and television production centre (after Los Angeles and New York).

Left: **Cruise Ship Passing Brockton Point**

A cruise ship bound for Alaska treats passengers to stunning urban views as it leaves Vancouver for the wilderness scenery of the North Pacific coast.

Raccoon

Emerging from the security of dense trailside shrubbery, the raccoons in Stanley Park have learned how to charm handouts from visitors. In the suburbs, their nimble hands lead them to a life of backyard burglary.

Tufted Duck Wintering on Lost Lagoon

This Eurasian duck took the wrong turn in Siberia and ended up on this side of the Pacific Rim, much to the delight of birdwatchers. Over 360 bird species have been recorded in Greater Vancouver.

Third Beach

This last sandy beach on the west shore ends near Siwash Rock, a park landmark thought by the Coast Salish to have special powers. Some of the park's big trees are in the forest above, including the largest red alder and bigleaf maple trees in Canada.

Right: Sunset, Seawall near Second Beach

Carved into cliffs and winding past sandy beaches, construction of the nine-kilometre seawall around Stanley Park was started in 1917 but not completed until 1980.

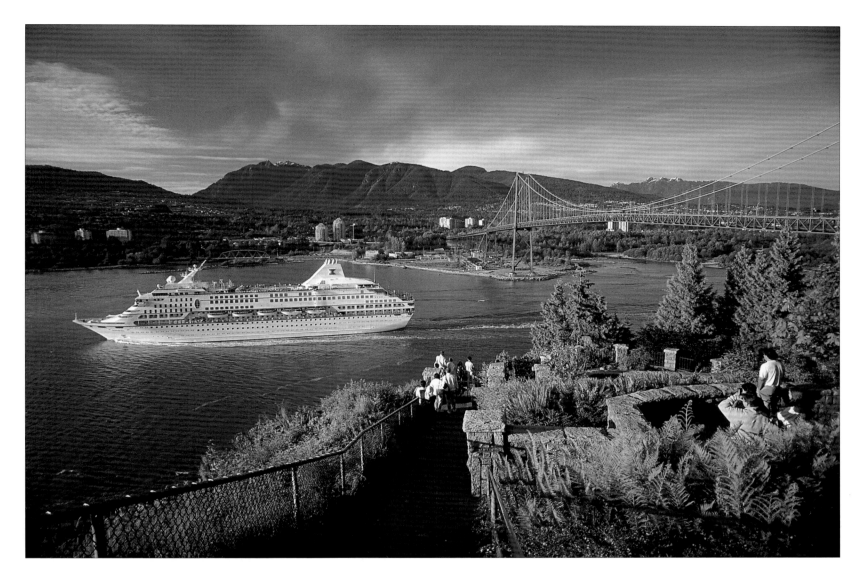

Cruise Ship below Prospect Point

This highest point in Stanley Park offers a bird's-eye view of the hundreds of cruise ships that depart from Vancouver to Alaska every summer. Seabirds nest on the cliffs below.

Left: **Lion's Gate Bridge**

Completed in 1938, this venerable landmark spanning the First Narrows has become a rush-hour bottleneck. Proposals for a new crossing range from twinning the bridge to building tunnels. Any new incursions in the park are fiercely resisted by the park's protectors.

The Fish House at Stanley Park

One of many superb restaurants serving fresh seafood, this one sits on the edge of the park, adjacent to the tennis courts and lawn bowling greens. The yellowing grass at the end of this long dry summer provides photographic evidence that "rainy Vancouver" often isn't.

Right: **Winter at Lost Lagoon**

A rare dusting of snow gives the ducks of Lost Lagoon a mild taste of real winter. Vancouver has only a 6 percent chance of having a white Christmas.

Rowing Lessons on Coal Harbour

The park's shoreline has been home to the Royal Vancouver Yacht Club and the Vancouver Rowing Club since the turn of the century. Ignoring the impending storm, these novices may be dreaming of joining the roster of Olympic rowers who first paddled here.

Left: **Coal Harbour from the Vancouver Rowing Club**

This 1911 heritage building offers a unique vantage point for fiery sunsets.

EAST SIDE/WEST SIDE

Vancouver City Hall

Watching over the downtown core from Mount Pleasant, one of Vancouver's oldest residential neighbourhoods, this distinctive building was a Depression-era project (1935-36). Its imposing architecture has been described as "totalitarian" — in sharp contrast to the spirit of the city.

Left: **Winter Joggers at Kitsilano Beach**

EAST SIDE/WEST SIDE

Vancouver is a city of neighbourhoods, each one with its own unique personality. From the lively mix of industry, ethnic communities and bohemians on the East Side around to the lush tranquillity of the University of British Columbia campus, the neighbourhoods of Vancouver are rich and varied. Along Burrard Inlet east from downtown to the Second Narrows Bridge, container terminals, a sugar refinery, giant grain elevators and other industrial buildings crowd the waterfront. But just a block away, mixed residential and commercial neighbourhoods stretch south to the Fraser River.

On the eastern border of Vancouver, Exhibition Park is the site of the Pacific National Exhibition every summer from mid-August to Labour Day. Cotton candy, agricultural exhibits and a midway blend with famous-name entertainment, monster-truck meets, demonstrations of logging prowess and arts, craft and cultural exhibits for an eclectic end-of-summer tradition. The PNE shares the park with a 5.5 furlong racetrack, a summer amusement park, and Empire Stadium, where Roger Bannister ran the Miracle Mile (under four minutes) in 1954.

In the heart of the Grandview neighbourhood, west of Exhibition Park, Commercial Drive has an atmosphere that's old world and new hip combined. The established Italian neighbourhood still thrives, evident in the best cappuccino and pizza in town, and in Victoria Park, where men play boccie. But life on the Drive gets its fizz from the blend of immigrant cultures that now includes those from Asia and Latin America and a social mix that includes young hipsters, aging hippies and anyone who doesn't wear a suit.

To the southeast, Mount Pleasant is a transition neighbourhood that serves as a bridge between the commercial/industrial/residential East Side and the upscale West Side. The city's lively arts community comes into its own every September with the Vancouver Fringe Festival, which draws theatre goers from across the city to Mount Pleasant.

No part of Vancouver has undergone more dramatic transformations than False Creek, northeast of Mount Pleasant. Little more than a century ago, it was a forested, marshy inlet filled with fish and wildlife. Then came rail yards, industry (including 17 sawmills) and landfills, creating a smoky, working harbour. Today it is beautiful once again, this time as a trendy and recreational waterfront.

In contrast to False Creek, Vancouver's West Side neighbourhoods are a picture of orderly planning. Surveyed in 1905, Kitsilano quickly became one of the most popular districts. One of its assets is Kitsilano Beach, part of 16 kilometres of sandy beaches that stretch from English Bay to Point Grey and Canada's first golf course at Jericho beach. These beaches pulled development westward, and in the 1960s, helped make Vancouver the "hippie capital" of Canada — a description that still fits Jericho Beach every summer at the Vancouver Folk Festival. This shoreline also hosts the Vancouver Children's Festival at Vanier Park, much of the Sea Festival at Kitsilano and Spanish Banks beaches, and some of the city's best views of the annual "Symphony of Fire" international fireworks competition.

At the far west point of the West Side lies the lush green campus of the University of British Columbia. In 1923, the huge, undeveloped government reserve on Point Grey was set aside as endowment lands for the benefit of the fledgling University of British Columbia. Sixty-six years later, in 1989, 763 hectares of these endowment lands became Pacific Spirit Regional Park. Wilder, quieter and twice as large as Stanley Park, the park has 50 kilometres of walking, cycling and horse trails meandering along shoreline cliffs, beaches and magnificent forests.

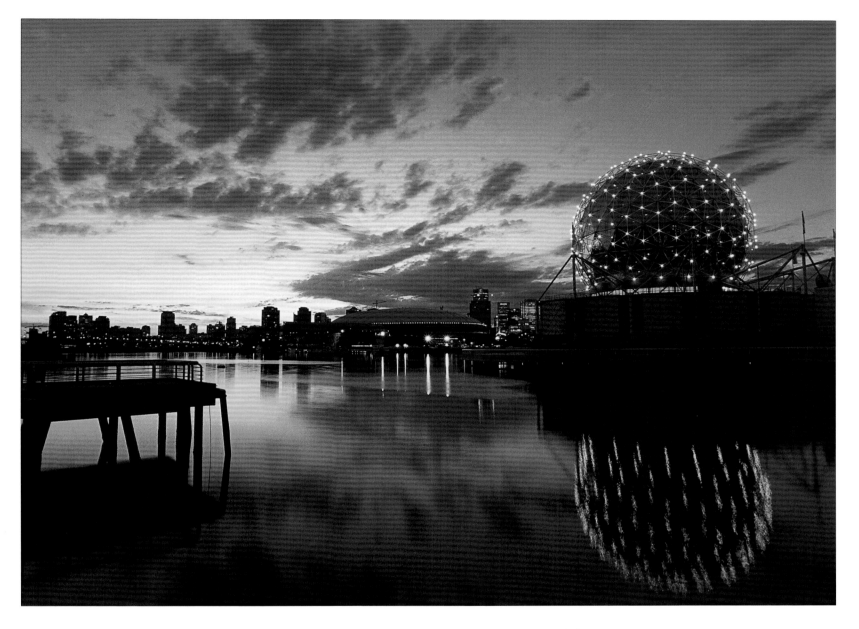

False Creek Sunset and Science World

This futuristic 15-storey stainless-steel geodesic "golf ball" at the head of False Creek was the Expo 86 Preview Centre and is now Science World. Filled with school groups in season, it is an interactive science museum with a wraparound theatre.

Granville Island Public Market

Since opening in 1979, this waterfront market with 100 independent merchants has been a fun place to shop. Fresh air, fresh ideas, fresh produce and, here, Fraser River sockeye salmon, fresh off the boat, delight local shoppers and tourists alike.

Left: Aerial View of False Creek and Granville Island

Spanned here by the Burrard Street Bridge across its mouth and the Granville Street Bridge above Granville Island, lower False Creek is becoming a new city centre. Aquabuses ferry commuters and shoppers to and from downtown and the West End.

False Creek Harbour and Concord Pacific Place

Beyond the boats stand some of the 1800 residences of the Beach neighbourhood, part of the $3-billion project rising on the north shore of False Creek. This meticulously planned "people place," with 20 hectares of parkland and 2.5 kilometres of seawall, will have double the population density of the West End.

Right: **False Creek**

In 20 years, False Creek has been transformed from an industrial eyesore to one of Vancouver's most beautiful neighbourhoods — and one of Canada's preferred addresses.

Rapid Transit

Commuters on the SkyTrain catch a glimpse of Molson Indy Vancouver. Chasing over $20 million in prize money on a 2.7-kilometre track around BC Place, the roaring engines can be heard across the city every Labour Day weekend (the first weekend in September).

Midway at Pacific National Exhibition

A million people attend this late-summer 17-day fair held in east Vancouver's Exhibition Park. Begun in 1910 as the Vancouver Exhibition, it still has a folksy "country fair" feeling.

Overleaf: **Winter Panorama from Mount Pleasant**

The traffic streaks down Cambie Street, past new condo and office developments and BC Place to downtown's bright lights. Twinkling on the North Shore horizon are the night-skiing lights of Cypress Bowl, near The Lions, and Grouse Mountain.

Nanaimo to Vancouver Bathtub Race

In the most famous event in the city's summer Sea Festival, this pilot must still run up Kitsilano Beach to the finish line — on legs cramped and wobbly after a long bouncing bathtub ride across the Strait of Georgia.

Summer Evening, Kitsilano Beach

Amateur and aspiring entertainers have been performing at the Kitsilano Showboat since 1935. The saltwater pool beyond dates back to 1931, and the sandy beaches have been here since long before Chief Khatsahlano's people lived here.

Beach Volleyball at Jericho Beach

Summer life is a beach for many Vancouverites. A 16-kilometre string of beaches lines the West Side. Kitsilano, Jericho, Locarno, Spanish Banks and Wreck beaches (the city's secluded nude beach) all enjoy an abundance of sand courtesy of the Fraser River, whose sediments are swept around Point Grey and deposited here.

February Morning, Vanier Park

These Canada Geese were probably as surprised as Vancouverites to find the city covered with snow this morning. Most cars are without snow tires so the city will have to wait a few hours — or perhaps a few days — to return to its normal pace.

H.R. Macmillan Planetarium

Designed in the shape of the cedar hats worn by the Coast Salish peoples, this dramatic landmark in Vanier Park has a domed theatre where the wonders of the universe are projected and music and laser productions are created. Visitors can see the real thing through a powerful telescope at the adjacent Gordon Southam Observatory. The attached Vancouver Museum offers a panorama of the city's past.

Right: West End and English Bay from Hadden Park

On this crisp winter day, the North Shore mountains seem close enough to touch. The point in the foreground shelters Heritage Harbour, the Vancouver Maritime Museum's outdoor exhibit.

Cherry Blossom Time, Arbutus Neighbourhood

As snowflakes fall in the rest of Canada, flower petals begin carpeting Vancouver. From March through May, a succession of blooms — on 19,000 flowering cherry trees, 14,000 white plums, 1600 magnolias, 1400 dogwoods, and many other flowering trees — fill residential streets with colour and scent.

University of British Columbia Library

Although UBC was officially established in 1908, it took 17 years and the "Great Trek" student march in 1922 before the campus finally opened in 1925. The library's stone core was built in 1923, and like the rest of the university, has greatly expanded since then. UBC is now Canada's third largest university, with over 40,000 students and leading research scientists.

The Raven and the First Men

This stunning cedar sculpture by acclaimed Haida artist Bill Reid, portrays the Haida myth of the creation of human beings: the raven, a mythical hero, creator and trickster, rests on the clamshell while the first people struggle to get out.

Right: **Museum of Anthropology**

Completed in 1976 to celebrate the historic and contemporary artistic achievements of the First Peoples of the North Pacific coast, this powerful building was designed by famous Vancouver architect Arthur Erickson, inspired by the cedar houses of the Coast Salish. Rising from the rim of the Point Grey cliffs adjacent to UBC, it displays a fabulous collection of Native art and offers exhibits, performances and educational programs.

Pacific Spirit Regional Park

This 763-hectare park around the UBC campus has 50 kilometres of trails leading to bogs, beaches, cliffs and forests. Here the sun plays on leaves beneath a towering canopy of Douglas firs.

Right: **Nitobe Memorial Garden**

Created in 1960 and carefully renewed in 1994, this authentic Japanese walled garden is a serene enclave, with every tree, stone and pathway artfully arranged to create a symbolic journey through the cycle of life. A place for peaceful meditations, its abstract meanings should be understood gradually, but its soothing beauty can be appreciated immediately.

Queen Elizabeth Park

Although the idea of indoor gardens might seem redundant on a spring day like this, the Bloedel Conservatory on the park's summit houses 500 species of tropical plants and exotic birds beneath its aluminum and Plexiglas dome.

Left: Wedding Party at Queen Elizabeth Park

Providing an ideal setting for countless wedding photographs, this garden (like the renowned Butchart Gardens of Victoria) was created out of a spent rock quarry, where basalt was crushed for roads until 1908.

Downtown from Queen Elizabeth Park

Perched atop the highest point in the city, 150-metre Little Mountain, the park affords sweeping views of the city. Here a breaking storm illuminates the skyline and the white dome of BC Place.

Left: Great Blue Heron, VanDusen Botanical Gardens

Although this diverse 22-hectare park was not created for them, these 90-centimetre birds (which nest in Pacific Spirit and Stanley parks) hunt the seven ponds here. For human visitors, there are 6500 plant species from six continents, a spectacular springtime Rhododendron Walk, a Victorian hedge maze and paths through peaceful places.

Rolls-Royces at the All-British Field Meet

One of the spring rites for car lovers from all over the Pacific Northwest is this gathering of British cars — especially classic sports cars — on the upper lawns of VanDusen Botanical Gardens.

Right: **Home on West Marine Drive**

Vancouver's British heritage is evident in the stately Tudor mansions, with their English green grounds, that can be found in Shaughnessy, West Point Grey and University Hill.

NORTH SHORE

Vancouver Panorama from West Vancouver

With views like this, it is easy to see why wealthy residents flocked to this slope when the Lions Gate Bridge made downtown Vancouver easily accessible.

Left: **Sunset from Mount Seymour**

The lights of the Lions Gate Bridge and the freighters waiting to enter Burrard Inlet compete with a fiery sunset over the Strait of Georgia and distant Vancouver Island.

NORTH SHORE

When the creative minds in downtown Vancouver came up with Tourism British Columbia's classic "Super, Natural" theme, they may have been gazing across Burrard Inlet to the North Shore. There they could see West and North Vancouver climbing the spectacular North Shore mountains, where civilized superlatives — some of Canada's finest residences, home to Canada's wealthiest population — boldly contrast with wild, beautiful nature. The top streets mark the sudden edge of the vast rugged Coast Mountain wilderness that stretches north to Alaska — an edge so sudden that deer, black bears and the occasional mountain lion wander into town.

While Vancouverites could both sail and ski on a winter day, North Shore residents could easily do both in an afternoon — with time left for shopping, scuba diving or a night out. There are three ski areas on the mountains directly above them: Cypress Provincial Park, Grouse Mountain, and Mount Seymour Provincial Park. With their stupendous views, all are popular for hiking, cycling and sightseeing when the snow melts.

In West Vancouver, the mountains rise steeply from a narrow rocky shoreline. Before the Lions Gate Bridge was built in 1938, this community was little more than a string of waterfront cottages along a winding Marine Drive. Since the bridge's construction, West Vancouver has been luring residents with panoramic views of Burrard Inlet and the Vancouver region. At its sunny far western point, West Vancouver has some of Canada's most innovative residential architecture — archetypal "West Coast style" — in cliffside niches above the sailboats in Eagle Harbour, around Horseshoe Bay and adjacent to Whytecliff Park on Howe Sound.

To the east, the rolling slopes and broad waterfront of North Vancouver were the site of the oldest community on Burrard Inlet. In the 1860s, Moodyville was a progressive town — the first library, newspaper, and school on Burrard Inlet — where Sewell P. Moody's millworkers could live peaceful, productive and dry lives, aloof from the rowdiness at Gastown. While Vancouver boomed with the coming of the railway, North Vancouver remained a quiet place apart, hemmed in by mountains and accessible only by boat until 1925.

Although linked to Vancouver by two bridges and the SeaBus, North and West Vancouver still retain their distinctive small-city feel. Strolling the waterfront at Lonsdale Quay or when easily finding a place to park, visitors may feel that downtown Vancouver seems worlds away. And if North and West Vancouver seem too urban, a short drive east is the village of Deep Cove on Indian Arm in a setting that looks, feels and sounds like a remote coastal fjord.

Right: **SeaBus and Vancouver Skyline**

With both the Second Narrows and Lions Gate Bridges being bottlenecks in rush hour, many North Vancouver commuters prefer this short cruise across Burrard Inlet to downtown.

Overleaf: **North Vancouver and the North Shore Mountains**

Lonsdale Quay Public Market

North Vancouver's waterfront people place opened in 1985 in the midst of an industrial waterfront at the foot of Lonsdale Avenue. Adjacent to the SeaBus terminal, it offers decks to watch the little ferries come and go, restaurants, a hotel and a large public market. Right next door, a tugboat port and shipyard go right on working.

Left: **Lonsdale Avenue, North Vancouver**

North Vancouver's steep main street affords views of busy Burrard Inlet and the SeaBuses ferrying commuters to downtown Vancouver.

Waterfront Park, North Vancouver

One of the few green spaces on the city's working waterfront, this quiet park is just steps away from the busy SeaBus terminal and Lonsdale Quay.

Right: **Capilano Suspension Bridge**

This swaying bridge has been a famous tourist attraction since the first rope and plank bridge was strung across the Capilano River canyon in 1889. Today's 137-metre steel-cable bridge is 69 metres above the river. Firmly anchored in tons of concrete, it still thrills visitors when it swings. A smaller bridge swings above Lynn Canyon farther east.

Night Skier's View from Grouse Mountain

The 1250-metre summit of Grouse Mountain offers striking views of the Vancouver region, especially at sunset.

Right: **Cedar Hikers, Grouse Mountain Skyride**

Although some people hike (or bike) from here to the summit, most take the 8-minute, 1128-metre glide up the Skyride gondola, rising through the clouds above these carvings. There they find a mountaintop resort and a glorious view of the Vancouver region.

Lighthouse Park, West Vancouver

At the southwestern tip of West Vancouver, this lighthouse on Point Atkinson has been guiding ships since 1914. Untouched since first reserved in 1881, this 75-hectare park also holds a magnificent old growth forest of giant Douglas firs.

Right: **Ambleside Park, West Vancouver**

Ambleside Park has West Vancouver's only big sandy beach, formed by the delta of the Capilano River. The river also brings coho salmon, returning to spawn. For countless generations, this was a Squamish fishing camp. Enhanced by a fish hatchery, and despite all the urban changes, anglers can still catch coho salmon at the river's mouth.

Upper Levels Highway, West Vancouver

Completed in the 1950s, this stretch of the Trans-Canada Highway provides rapid access across the North Shore to these homes on Eagle Ridge. Beyond are the Horseshoe Bay ferry to Vancouver Island and the Sea to Sky Highway to the resorts of Whistler.

Left: **North Shore Mountains, Cypress Provincial Park**

Moist Pacific air pushed up these slopes brings clouds and greater precipitation — 50 percent more than on the western shoreline below and twice as much as on the foreshore of the Fraser River delta.

Previous page: **Winter Sunset from West Vancouver**

Eagle Harbour

With their yachts and sailboats safely moored in sheltered Eagle Harbour, some of the "Who's Who" of Canada enjoy awesome views from their magnificent homes perched high on the slopes above.

Right: **Whytecliff Park**

On a rocky point in the mouth of Howe Sound, this park is a favourite site for scuba divers exploring the rich and varied marine life in the underwater reserve.

Royal Hudson Steam Train

This last working steam locomotive in Canada pulls trainloads of sight-seeing tourists from North Vancouver up the shoreline of spectacular Howe Sound to Squamish each summer. Passengers can return by train or on a boat cruise.

Right: **Horseshoe Bay, Howe Sound**

This busy port serves large ferries that travel to Vancouver Island and smaller ones that cross Howe Sound to the Sunshine Coast and Bowen Island, 20 minutes offshore. A summer cottage resort since the turn of the century, Bowen Island today is home to daily commuters to downtown Vancouver.

BEYOND VANCOUVER

Whistler

Consistently rated the top ski and winter resort in North America, Whistler is also a summer playground. The resort sprawls in the lake-dotted Pemberton Valley, beneath two huge mountains on the western edge of Garibaldi Provincial Park, one of BC's oldest parks.

Left: **Bridal Falls**

These falls spilling down a mountain slope south of Chilliwack are but one of countless natural beauty spots in the region. Despite the Fraser Valley's tremendous recent population growth, the rugged landscape that surrounds it keeps civilization at bay.

BEYOND VANCOUVER

Mountains and water — both salt and fresh — create Vancouver's dramatic setting, shaping the city and its neighbouring communities. Where salt and fresh water meet at the Fraser Delta, rich farmland feels the pressures of intense urban development. Eastward, the Fraser Valley becomes more "wild west" than "big city." The annual rodeo at Cloverdale is the second largest professional rodeo in Canada. The valley's fertile fields sprout every type of crop from corn to daffodils, as dairy cattle munch sedately in the shadow of the Coast Mountains.

Of the 1.7 million people who live in Greater Vancouver, only 500,000 live in the City of Vancouver. The rest swell the other municipalities of the Lower Mainland, which together make this the fastest growing region in Canada. On Vancouver's eastern border is the city of Burnaby. The best view in town is of Vancouver from Burnaby Mountain, the hilltop home of Simon Fraser University. Its modern campus was designed by the internationally known architect Arthur Erickson.

To the southeast is the first capital of British Columbia, New Westminster. Because its name was personally chosen by Queen Victoria, New Westminster has been known as the "Royal City" since it was established in 1858. Today its beautiful heritage homes overlook the busy Fraser River from bluffs once valued by the military for their strategic location.

Sprawling Surrey, also to the southeast of Vancouver, dwarfs the other communities of the Lower Mainland. With town centres in Newton, Whalley, Guildford, Cloverdale and Sunnyside, it is the fastest growing municipality in Canada. Surrey extends all the way to the Canada–United States border, but it's not wall-to-wall suburbs. It includes industrial parks, lush farmlands, golf courses, and some of the best beaches in the Lower Mainland at White Rock and Crescent Beach.

Richmond, due south of Vancouver, is built on the islands of the Fraser River. Once prone to flooding, its flat landscape (averaging only two metres above sea level) is protected by an extensive system of dikes. Another booming municipality, Richmond has a growing Asian community, many from Hong Kong. In the quiet southwest corner of the municipality lies the picturesque fishing village of Steveston. Once home to more than a dozen canneries, it even had an opera house! Now a quiet backwater, it's still a great place to buy fresh fish.

South of Richmond and reaching to the Canada-United States border at Point Roberts is the municipality of Delta. Like many of the other large municipalities around Vancouver, Delta is a collection of smaller communities — Ladner, North Delta and Tsawwassen — mixed with agricultural land, industry and parks. Delta's large areas of wetlands attract huge bird populations and, in turn, large numbers of bird watchers from all over the Lower Mainland.

For those tired of the hustle and bustle of the Lower Mainland, two completely different resorts offer respite. East of Vancouver, Harrison Hot Springs can soothe weary bodies. North of Vancouver, Whistler offers another kind of relaxation. Just two decades ago, skiers drove a rough logging road from Squamish to very basic facilities on Whistler Mountain. In 1975, the provincial government created Whistler Village, Canada's first and only resort municipality. Since then, Whistler has become the top-rated ski destination on the continent, with two huge mountains and long runs down the greatest skiable vertical relief in North America. With five lakes, golf courses, tennis schools and the Vancouver Symphony performing on the mountain top, it's becoming a summer place to match.

Furry Creek Golf Course, Howe Sound

With a year-round season and a rapidly growing number of players, the Vancouver region is sprouting golf courses almost as fast as new homes. Golfing began in Vancouver in 1905, at Jericho Beach. Following that oceanside tradition, this new course straddles the Sea to Sky Highway between Porteau Cove Provincial Park and the old mining town of Britannia Beach.

Fraser River Bridges, New Westminster

The "Royal City" was chosen as the colonial capital in 1858 because of the military advantage of its bluffs above the Fraser River. Later these bluffs became an ideal base for bridges. Trains first crossed in 1904; the orange Pattullo Bridge opened for traffic in 1937; and the SkyBridge began carrying SkyTrain commuters across to Surrey in 1990.

Right: **Tour Boat on Harrison Lake**

The popularity of the resort town of Harrison Hot Springs has made this view famous. Glacier-capped Mt. Breakenridge is in the distance. Harrison Lake is the largest of several fjord-like lakes — Coquitlam, Pitt, Alouette, Stave and Chehalis — filling Coast Mountain valleys north of the Fraser River.

Sunny White Rock

Far from the cloudy mountains, this sunniest beach in the Vancouver region has been a popular summer resort since the Great Northern Railway arrived in 1909. Today many summer cottages have been replaced by exclusive homes.

Steveston, South Arm of the Fraser River

This quaint fishing port in Richmond has developed a neighbourhood of trendy shops and seafood eateries above the public docks, where customers can buy salmon fresh off the boat. Once a largely Japanese village, Steveston is becoming a major attraction with the development of the Gulf of Georgia Cannery National Historic Site.

Snow Geese at George C. Reifel Waterfowl Refuge, Ladner

With Mount Baker in Washington State looming in the background, some of the 25,000 snow geese that stop here on their way south from their Siberian nesting grounds glide down to a field of potatoes planted for their benefit. Sights and sounds alike — enjoyed by thousands at the refuge's annual Snow Goose Festival — remind us of the ecological richness of the Vancouver region.